All about Dad and Me

all about DAD and ME

A Journal for Fathers and Daughters

Illustrated by Mariia Kolker

ROCKRIDGE
PRESS

Interior and Cover Designer: Lisa Schreiber
Art Producer: Samantha Ulban
Editor: Eun H. Jeong
Production Editor: Jax Berman
Production Manager: Riley Hoffman

Illustrations © 2022 Mariia Kolker.

Paperback ISBN: 978-1-63878-102-8
R0

This journal belongs to:

_____
FATHER

and

_____
DAUGHTER

Getting on the Same Page

Welcome to *All about Dad and Me: A Journal for Fathers and Daughters*! From sharing embarrassing moments to describing your perfect day, this journal is an opportunity for the two of you as father and daughter to learn more about each other in a fun and creative way. For the daughters, maybe you'll find out that your dad also hated broccoli as a kid. For the dads, perhaps you'll be pleasantly surprised to discover that your child's favorite memory is not what you would have guessed.

Before you begin writing, we encourage you to sit down and talk about how, exactly, this process will work. To make it easier, we'll share some guidelines that you can discuss together. If you just can't wait to start writing, it's okay to skip this part and jump right in! The "right" way to use this journal is whatever works best for the two of you.

Is This a Secret?

Something you may want to talk about is who else, if anyone, will be allowed to see this journal. If you decide it's just for the two of you, then you may need to brainstorm a great hiding spot to keep it safe from nosy family members and friends!

Speaking of nosy family members and friends, will you allow each other to talk about the journal with anyone else? Or will you pinky-swear that it'll be a father-daughter secret forever? It's important that you both agree on this particular point; otherwise, there may be trouble if a curious aunt, cousin, or close family friend mentions it over a holiday gathering or birthday dinner.

Filling Out Entries

What about filling out the entries themselves? Perhaps one of you is systematic and organized and would naturally fill out the journal in order, and the other is more spontaneous and would like to write about whatever topic seems appealing at the moment. Does one of you choose the prompt on odd days and the other on even days? Discuss the best way to handle this so that you are both (literally!) on the same page.

Passing the Journal Back and Forth

Discuss how the journal will be passed back and forth. If the journal is being kept top secret, do you have different nightly drop locations and code names, as if you were in your own father-daughter spy movie? Or will you simply leave it on each other's nightstands when you are done? If one of you is traveling somewhere, or you live in different places from each other, get creative with how you'll pass it back and forth. You could write in it either when you spend time together or hand it off during the times when you're apart so that each of you has some time to spend with your entries! Do whatever works best for both of you.

Setting a Schedule

Finally, talk about timing. Will you write in the journal every day? Once a week? Once the journal is passed to the other person, will there be a certain amount of time before you have to return it? Or maybe it will be totally flexible. Some days will be busier than others, and some days you just may not feel like writing at all. That's okay. Think of the journal as a marathon, not a sprint. This is a keepsake you'll have for many years, so taking care and time with it will only make it more valuable for both of you.

Keep in Mind

Here are some ideas to keep in mind when writing your entries.

Be Honest

Remember, this journal is a safe space in which to share your feelings. The purpose of this experience is to develop a deeper understanding of each other, and being honest with your words and feelings is the best way to do that. Keeping an open mind when using this journal will ensure that both of you feel respected.

Listen to Each Other

There is an opportunity here to really listen to each other. With our everyday schedules, we aren't always able to give people our full attention at the exact moment they want it. We all get busy, whether it's doing homework, making dinner, or finishing chores, and that's totally understandable. But when you hand each other something you've written, think of it as a signal to take a moment (when you can!) to read it, and to pay attention to what each other has to say. If there's one thing that fathers and daughters have in common, it's that they both want to feel heard.

Have Fun

Above all else, this journal should be a fun activity for the two of you to share. Don't be afraid to be silly, creative, or think outside the box. In the drawing section, some of you dads might find out that your artistic abilities peaked at around the fourth grade. Some of you daughters might find out drawing is your new favorite creative hobby! One of you might like to be wildly colorful, and the other one might be into black-and-white scribbles. That's okay! No matter how you each express yourself, being the "true you" is most important. Sharing this space should never feel like a "have-to"; if there are times when one of you is just not feeling it, then step away for a while. We promise, the journal won't be offended, and it will still be there when you are inspired to write again.

Tell Stories

Every family has their stories. Some are funny, some are sad, some might make you howl until you've got tears running down your cheeks, and some are just bound to be a little bit embarrassing. No matter what you get out of each story, enjoy the telling and learn from it together. Sharing stories provides entertainment, unites us as fathers and daughters, and gives us a deeper understanding of our past, our hopes, and what we want for our futures. This journal's prompts will make it easy to transfer those stories from your memory to the page, where they can be relived over and over for many years to come.

Father

Describe three things you admire about your daughter.

1 _____

_____

_____

2 _____

_____

_____

3 _____

_____

_____

» Daughter «

Describe three things you admire about your dad.

1 _____

_____

_____

2 _____

_____

_____

3 _____

_____

_____

What is your favorite season?

_____

What are four things you like about this time of year?

1 _____

_____

2 _____

_____

3 _____

_____

4 _____

_____

»Daughter«

What is your favorite season?

_____

What are four things you like about this time of year?

1 _____

_____

2 _____

_____

3 _____

_____

4 _____

_____

Did you have a favorite pet as a child? If you didn't have a pet, what pet would you choose if you could have had one and why?

_____

_____

_____

_____

_____

Do you have any stories about this pet?

_____

_____

_____

_____

_____

Do you have any pets? If yes, do you want any other pets? If no, do you want a pet?

_____

_____

_____

_____

What is your favorite thing about your pet? If you don't have a pet, what pet would you choose if you could have one, and why?

_____

_____

_____

_____

_____

What's the nicest thing a friend has ever done for you?

_____

_____

_____

_____

_____

What's the nicest thing you've ever done for a friend?

_____

_____

_____

_____

_____

Daughter

What's the nicest thing a friend has ever done for you?

_____

_____

_____

_____

What's the nicest thing you've ever done for a friend?

_____

_____

_____

_____

What would you do if you could trade places with your daughter for a day?

_____

_____

_____

_____

_____

_____

_____

_____

_____

_____

» Daughter «

What would you do if you could trade places with your dad for a day?

_____

_____

_____

_____

_____

_____

_____

_____

_____

_____

» Father «

If you could rule the world for a day, what exactly would you do?

_____

_____

_____

_____

_____

_____

_____

_____

_____

_____

» Daughter «

If you could rule the world for a day, what exactly would you do?

_____

_____

_____

_____

_____

_____

_____

_____

_____

_____

Father

In what ways are you most similar to your daughter?

_____

_____

_____

_____

_____

In what ways are you most different?

_____

_____

_____

_____

_____

» Daughter «

How are you and your dad alike?

_____

_____

_____

_____

_____

_____

How are you and your dad different?

_____

_____

_____

_____

_____

What was your very first job? How much did you get paid?

_____

_____

_____

_____

_____

What did you learn from this job?

_____

_____

_____

_____

_____

» Daughter «

If you could have a job right now, what would you want to do?

_____

_____

_____

_____

What would you do with the money you made?

_____

_____

_____

_____

» Father «

Who is the person you find easiest to talk to? Why did you choose this person?

_____

_____

_____

_____

_____

Who do you trust the most?

_____

_____

_____

_____

_____

_____

» Daughter «

Who is the person you find easiest to talk to? Why did you choose this person?

_____

_____

_____

Who do you trust the most?

_____

_____

_____

Who is the person you would trust the most with a secret?

_____

_____

_____

What is the best gift you've ever received?

_____

_____

_____

_____

What is the best gift you've ever given someone?

_____

_____

_____

_____

Daughter

What is the best gift you've ever received?

_____

_____

_____

_____

What is the best gift you've ever given someone?

_____

_____

_____

_____

_____

» Father «

Describe your daughter in five words.

1 _____

2 _____

3 _____

4 _____

5 _____

Describe yourself in five words.

1 _____

2 _____

3 _____

4 _____

5 _____

» Daughter «

Describe your dad in five words.

1 _____

2 _____

3 _____

4 _____

5 _____

Describe yourself in five words.

1 _____

2 _____

3 _____

4 _____

5 _____

» Father «

Who is your favorite TV family?

_____

_____

_____

_____

What are the qualities you admire about them?

_____

_____

_____

_____

_____

_____

» Daughter «

Who is your favorite TV family?

_____

_____

_____

_____

Do you think it would be fun to be a part of this family? Why or why not?

_____

_____

_____

_____

Father

Who was your favorite teacher as a child? Why?

_____

_____

_____

What was your favorite subject in school?

_____

_____

_____

What was your least-favorite subject in school?

_____

_____

_____

Daughter

Who is your favorite teacher?

_____

_____

What is the best thing about this teacher?

_____

_____

What is your favorite subject in school?

_____

_____

What is your least-favorite subject in school?

_____

_____

» Father «

Things that make you laugh:

_____

_____

Things that make you cry:

_____

_____

Things that make you proud:

_____

_____

Things that make you excited:

_____

_____

» Daughter «

Things that make you laugh:

_____

_____

Things that make you cry:

_____

_____

Things that make you proud:

_____

_____

Things that make you excited:

_____

_____

» Father «

What was your favorite vacation as a child?

_____

_____

_____

_____

Who did you go with, and what did you do there?

_____

_____

_____

_____

_____

_____

What is the best vacation you've been on?

_____

_____

_____

If you could pick any vacation spot, what would it be?

_____

_____

_____

Who would you bring on vacation with you?

_____

_____

_____

Father

What is the best thing about your family?

_____

_____

_____

_____

_____

What is the most unusual thing about your family?

_____

_____

_____

_____

_____

_____

Daughter

What is the best thing about your family?

_____

_____

_____

_____

What is the most unusual thing about your family?

_____

_____

_____

_____

» Father «

Draw a portrait of your daughter:

» Daughter «

Draw a portrait of your dad:

≫ Father ≪

Write about a time you got in trouble.

_____

_____

_____

_____

What did you learn from that experience?

_____

_____

_____

_____

_____

≫ Daughter ≪

Write about a time you got in trouble.

_____

_____

_____

_____

What did you learn from that experience?

_____

_____

_____

_____

_____

» Father «

What is your favorite holiday?

_____

What are three reasons why this holiday is your favorite?

1 _____

2 _____

3 _____

What is your favorite memory of this holiday?

_____

_____

_____

_____

_____

» Daughter «

What is your favorite holiday?

_____

What are three reasons why this holiday is your favorite?

1 _____

2 _____

3 _____

What is your favorite memory of this holiday?

_____

_____

_____

_____

Father

What was your most embarrassing moment as a child?

_____

_____

_____

_____

When were you most proud of yourself as a child?

_____

_____

_____

_____

_____

Daughter

What was your most embarrassing moment?

_____

_____

_____

_____

_____

What was your proudest moment?

_____

_____

_____

_____

_____

» Father «

If you could have any superpower, what would it be?

_____

_____

_____

How would you use it to make the world a better place?

_____

_____

_____

_____

_____

_____

_____

» Daughter «

If you could have any superpower, what would it be?

_____

_____

_____

How would you use it to make the world a better place?

_____

_____

_____

_____

_____

_____

_____

» Father «

How did you spend your summer days as a child?

_____

_____

_____

_____

What things did you do that your daughter has not yet experienced?

_____

_____

_____

_____

_____

What's your favorite thing about summer?

_____

_____

_____

_____

What's one way summer could be better?

_____

_____

_____

_____

_____

✏ Father ✏

What is your favorite breakfast?

_____

What is your favorite kind of cookie?

_____

What is one food you never get tired of?

_____

What is the most unusual food you've ever eaten?

_____

What is one food you never want to eat again?

_____

Daughter

What is your favorite breakfast?

_____

What is your favorite kind of cookie?

_____

What is one food you never get tired of?

_____

What is the most unusual food you've ever eaten?

_____

What is one food you never want to eat again?

_____

»Father«

Describe a perfect day with your daughter.

_____

_____

_____

_____

»Daughter«

If you could plan a perfect day with your dad, where would you go and what would you do?

_____

_____

_____

_____

» Father «

What is your favorite birthday memory?

_____

_____

_____

What is the best birthday gift you've ever received?

_____

_____

_____

Have you ever had a surprise party? If not, would you want one? If so, share about it.

_____

_____

_____

» Daughter «

What is your favorite birthday memory?

_____

_____

_____

What is the best birthday gift you've ever received?

_____

_____

_____

Have you ever had a surprise party? If not, would you want one? If so, share about it.

_____

_____

_____

What is an outdoor activity you'd like to do with your daughter?

_____

_____

Make plans to do it together! Afterward, share your thoughts on how it went. What did you enjoy about it?

_____

_____

_____

_____

_____

_____

_____

_____

_____

Daughter

What is an outdoor activity you'd like to do with your dad?

_____

_____

Make plans to do it together! Afterward, share your thoughts on how it went. What did you enjoy about it?

_____

_____

_____

_____

_____

_____

_____

_____

» Father «

What is the best advice your parents ever gave you?

_____

_____

_____

_____

_____

If you could make your daughter follow one piece of advice, what would it be?

_____

_____

_____

_____

_____

_____

» Daughter «

What is the best advice your dad ever gave you?

_____

_____

_____

_____

If you could give your dad one piece of advice, what would it be?

_____

_____

_____

_____

Father

Name a leader who inspires you. What about them is inspiring?

_____

_____

_____

_____

What are the qualities that a leader should have?

_____

_____

_____

_____

_____

Daughter

Name a leader who inspires you. What about them is inspiring?

_____

_____

_____

_____

Would you want to be a leader? Why or why not?

_____

_____

_____

_____

_____

» Father «

You won the lottery! Draw how you would spend your money:

»Daughter«

You won the lottery! Draw how you would spend your money:

Father

What did you eat for breakfast as a child?

_____

_____

_____

Did you bring lunch to school, or did you buy lunch in the cafeteria?

_____

_____

_____

What was the best thing your parents made for dinner?

_____

_____

_____

What foods do you usually eat for breakfast?

_____

_____

_____

Would you rather bring or buy your lunch?

_____

_____

_____

What's your favorite thing to eat with your dad?

_____

_____

_____

» Father «

What is the best place you've ever been?

_____

_____

What are three reasons this place is special?

1 _____

_____

2 _____

_____

3 _____

_____

_____

» Daughter «

What is the best place you've ever been?

_____

_____

What are three reasons this place is special?

1 _____

_____

2 _____

_____

3 _____

_____

» Father «

What is one place you would like to go with your daughter?

_____

_____

_____

_____

_____

_____

_____

_____

_____

» Daughter «

What is one place you would like to go with your dad?

_____

_____

_____

_____

_____

_____

_____

_____

_____

# Father

When do you feel the strongest?

_____

_____

_____

_____

_____

When do you feel the weakest?

_____

_____

_____

_____

_____

Daughter

When do you feel the strongest?

_____

_____

_____

_____

_____

_____

When do you feel the weakest?

_____

_____

_____

_____

_____

» Father «

Did you fight with your siblings or other family members growing up? If so, what did you fight about?

_____

_____

_____

_____

Did you like being the only/oldest/middle/youngest child? Why?

_____

_____

_____

_____

» Daughter «

Do you fight with your siblings or other family members? If so, what do you fight about the most?

_____

_____

_____

_____

_____

Do you like being the only/oldest/middle/youngest child? Why?

_____

_____

_____

_____

_____

» Father «

What is your greatest talent?

_____

What are some talents you wish you had?

_____

_____

» Daughter «

What is your greatest talent?

_____

What are some talents you wish you had?

_____

_____

»» *Father* ««

Do you have a favorite grandparent?

_____

_____

_____

What is something they taught you?

_____

_____

_____

What is your favorite memory involving them?

_____

_____

_____

Daughter

What is the best thing about your grandparents?

_____

_____

_____

What is one thing your grandparents have taught you?

_____

_____

_____

What is your favorite memory involving your grandparents?

_____

_____

_____

» Father «

What is something your daughter does that makes you laugh?

_____

What's the funniest thing your daughter has ever said?

_____

» Daughter «

What is something your dad does that makes you laugh?

_____

What happened that made your dad laugh the most?

_____

If you could invent one thing, what would it be?

_____

_____

_____

Why do you think this invention is needed?

_____

_____

_____

_____

_____

_____

_____

If you could invent one thing, what would it be?

_____

_____

_____

Why do you think this invention is needed?

_____

_____

_____

_____

_____

_____

_____

» Father «

What was the hardest age for you growing up?

_____

What do you think would have made this age a little easier for you?

_____

_____

_____

_____

_____

_____

_____

_____

Daughter

If you could be any age, what age would you be?

_____

What do you think would be fun about being this age?

_____

_____

_____

_____

_____

_____

_____

_____

» Father «

Have you ever lost a friendship?

_____

_____

Do you regret losing that friendship? Is there something you could have done to fix the friendship?

_____

_____

_____

_____

_____

_____

_____

» Daughter «

Have you ever had a fight with a friend?

_____

_____

How could you handle the situation differently next time?

_____

_____

_____

_____

_____

_____

_____

_____

» Father «

What are three important things your daughter has taught you?

1 _____

2 _____

3 _____

» Daughter «

What are three important things your dad has taught you?

1 _____

2 _____

3 _____

Father

Who is the bravest person you know?

_____

What makes them brave?

_____

_____

_____

_____

_____

_____

_____

_____

_____

Daughter

Who is the bravest person you know?

_____

What makes them brave?

_____

_____

_____

_____

_____

_____

_____

_____

» Father «

The best part of being a dad is:

_____

_____

_____

_____

_____

The hardest part of being a dad is:

_____

_____

_____

_____

_____

» Daughter «

The best part of being a kid is:

_____

_____

_____

_____

_____

The hardest part of being a kid is:

_____

_____

_____

_____

_____

» Father «

What was your favorite book as a child?

_____

What was your daughter's favorite book when she was little?

_____

» Daughter «

What is your favorite book?

_____

If you wrote a book, what would the title be?

_____

Father

What famous person would you most like to meet?

_____

How would you spend a day with them?

_____

_____

_____

_____

_____

_____

_____

_____

_____

Daughter

What famous person would you most like to meet?

_____

How would you spend a day with them?

_____

_____

_____

_____

_____

_____

_____

_____

Father

Draw your dream house:

»Daughter«

Draw your dream house:

» Father «

What language would you like to learn?

_____

How would speaking this language benefit you?

_____

_____

_____

_____

_____

_____

_____

_____

» Daughter «

What language would you like to learn?

_____

How would speaking this language be helpful to you?

_____

_____

_____

_____

_____

_____

_____

_____

_____

» Father «

If you were granted three wishes, what would you wish for?

1 _____

2 _____

3 _____

» Daughter «

If you were granted three wishes, what would you wish for?

1 _____

2 _____

3 _____

Father

What's the biggest difference between your childhood and your daughter's childhood?

_____

_____

_____

_____

What are some things that are the same?

_____

_____

_____

_____

_____

_____

Daughter

What do you think your dad's childhood was like?

_____

_____

_____

_____

Do you think it was harder or easier than yours? Why?

_____

_____

_____

_____

_____

_____

_____

» Father «

What keeps you up at night worrying?

_____

_____

_____

_____

Why do you think this scares you?

_____

_____

_____

_____

_____

» Daughter «

What is something that worries you?

_____

_____

_____

_____

You would worry less about it if:

_____

_____

_____

_____

_____

» Father «

What has been your greatest accomplishment?

_____

_____

_____

_____

_____

What is something you would like to accomplish in the future?

_____

_____

_____

_____

_____

What has been your greatest accomplishment so far?

_____

_____

_____

_____

_____

What is something you'd like to accomplish in the future?

_____

_____

_____

_____

_____

_____

Father

Who was your best friend when you were your daughter's age?

_____

_____

_____

What are the qualities you liked most about them?

_____

_____

_____

What is your favorite memory involving them?

_____

_____

_____

Daughter

Who is your best friend?

_____

_____

_____

What are the things you like best about them?

_____

_____

_____

What are your favorite things to do together?

_____

_____

_____

» Father «

What did you want to be when you grew up?

_____

_____

_____

_____

_____

How is your life different from that now?

_____

_____

_____

_____

_____

» Daughter «

What do you want to be when you grow up?

_____

_____

_____

_____

What are some things you can do to achieve this?

_____

_____

_____

_____

_____

» Father «

What are three things you wish for your daughter?

1 _____

_____

_____

2 _____

_____

_____

3 _____

_____

_____

» Daughter «

What are three things you wish for your dad?

1 _____

_____

_____

2 _____

_____

_____

3 _____

_____

_____

» Father «

What is something your daughter doesn't know about you?

_____

_____

_____

_____

» Daughter «

What is something you think your dad doesn't know about you?

_____

_____

_____

_____

» Father «

What are some toys, books, or keepsakes you saved from your childhood?

_____

_____

_____

_____

_____

What is your favorite story about one of them?

_____

_____

_____

_____

_____

» Daughter «

What are some things that you want to keep forever?

_____

_____

_____

_____

_____

Why do you want to keep them?

_____

_____

_____

_____

_____

» Father «

What is something that is hard for you to talk about?

_____

_____

_____

_____

_____

What would make it easier for you to open up?

_____

_____

_____

_____

_____

Daughter

What is something that's hard for you to talk about?

_____

_____

_____

_____

_____

What would make it easier for you to open up?

_____

_____

_____

_____

» Father «

Draw your future self:

Daughter

Draw your future self:

What is a rainy-day activity you'd like to do with your daughter?

_____

_____

_____

Make plans to do it together! Afterward, share your thoughts on how it went. What did you enjoy about it?

_____

_____

_____

_____

_____

_____

_____

Daughter

What is a rainy-day activity you'd like to do with your dad?

_____

_____

_____

Make plans to do it together! Afterward, share your thoughts on how it went. What did you enjoy about it?

_____

_____

_____

_____

_____

_____

» Father «

Were your parents strict when you were growing up?

_____

_____

_____

Did you have to do chores?

_____

_____

_____

Did you get an allowance?

_____

_____

_____

» Daughter «

When is your dad strict?

_____

_____

_____

Are you responsible for any chores? If so, which ones?

_____

_____

_____

Do you think kids should get an allowance? Why or why not?

_____

_____

_____

» Father «

What is the best part of having siblings or cousins?

_____

_____

_____

_____

_____

What are your favorite things to do with your siblings or cousins?

_____

_____

_____

_____

_____

_____

Daughter

What is the best part of having siblings or cousins?

_____

_____

_____

_____

What are your favorite things to do with your siblings or cousins?

_____

_____

_____

_____

_____

⟫ Father ⟪

Describe what you think your life will be like in 20 years. Where will you be living? How will you spend your days?

_____

_____

_____

_____

_____

_____

What will your daughter be like in 20 years?

_____

_____

_____

_____

Daughter

Describe what you think your life will be like in 20 years. Where will you be living? How will you spend your days?

_____

_____

_____

_____

_____

What will your dad be like in 20 years?

_____

_____

_____

_____

» Father «

What are some things you can do to be a helpful member of society?

_____

_____

_____

_____

» Daughter «

What are some things you can do to be a helpful member of society?

_____

_____

_____

_____

» Father «

What is the best part of being a grown-up?

_____

_____

_____

_____

_____

What is the most challenging part of being a grown-up?

_____

_____

_____

_____

_____

» Daughter «

What's the best part of being a kid?

_____

_____

_____

_____

_____

What's the most challenging part of being a kid?

_____

_____

_____

_____

Father

If you could travel back in time to one year in your life, which year would it be?

_____

_____

_____

_____

What would you do differently during that year?

_____

_____

_____

_____

_____

_____

Daughter

If you could relive one day of your life over again, which day would it be?

_____

_____

_____

_____

What is something you would do differently on that day, and why?

_____

_____

_____

_____

_____

_____

_____

» **Father** «

What do you think your daughter's most prized possession is?

_____

_____

_____

_____

What is your most prized possession?

_____

_____

_____

_____

_____

_____

» Daughter «

What do you think your dad's most prized possession is?

_____

_____

_____

_____

What is your most prized possession?

_____

_____

_____

_____

_____

_____

» Father «

Who is your favorite singer/band?

_____

_____

What are some of your favorite songs?

_____

_____

_____

What was the best concert you've ever been to?

_____

Who is an artist your daughter likes, but you don't?

_____

»Daughter«

Who is your favorite singer/band?

_____

_____

What are some of your favorite songs?

_____

_____

_____

_____

If you could go to any concert, what would it be?

_____

Who is a singer you like, but your dad doesn't?

_____

✒ Father ✒

What are some qualities you admire most in other people?

_____

_____

_____

_____

What qualities do you think people admire about you?

_____

_____

_____

_____

_____

Daughter

What are some qualities you admire most in other people?

_____

_____

_____

_____

What qualities do you think people admire about you?

_____

_____

_____

_____

_____

Father

What's the best thing about the country you live in?

_____

_____

_____

_____

_____

What is a law that you would change?

_____

_____

_____

_____

_____

Daughter

What is the best thing about the country you live in?

_____

_____

_____

_____

_____

What is a law that you would change?

_____

_____

_____

_____

_____

» Father «

What was the coolest technology you had when you were a child?

_____

_____

_____

_____

_____

What is your favorite technology today?

_____

_____

_____

_____

_____

What do you think is the coolest technology now?

_____

_____

_____

_____

_____

What do you think technology will be like when you reach your dad's age?

_____

_____

_____

_____

Father

What makes you sad?

_____

_____

_____

_____

_____

What comforts you when you're sad?

_____

_____

_____

_____

_____

_____

Daughter

What makes you sad?

_____

_____

_____

_____

What comforts you when you're sad?

_____

_____

_____

_____

_____

» Father «

Who is the funniest person you know?

_____

Who is the most generous person you know?

_____

Who is the most hardworking person you know?

_____

Who can you always count on?

_____

Who do you argue with the most?

_____

» Daughter «

Who is the funniest person you know?

_____

Who is the most generous person you know?

_____

Who is the most hardworking person you know?

_____

Who can you always count on?

_____

Who do you argue with the most?

_____

» Father «

What was your favorite sport or game to play as a child?

_____

_____

_____

What did you like about it?

_____

_____

_____

What is your favorite sport or game now?

_____

_____

_____

» Daughter «

What is your favorite sport or game?

_____

_____

_____

What are some reasons you like to play it?

_____

_____

_____

What is a sport or game you'd like to learn?

_____

_____

_____

Father

How did your parents choose your name?

_____

_____

_____

_____

_____

If you could choose your own name, what would it be?

_____

_____

_____

_____

Daughter

Why did your parents choose your name?

_____

_____

_____

If you could choose a name for yourself, what would it be?

_____

_____

_____

If you have a child someday, what will you name them?

_____

_____

_____

» Father «

If you were stranded on a desert island, which three people would you want with you?

_____

_____

_____

How would these people make your experience on the island easier or better?

_____

_____

_____

_____

_____

_____

_____

_____

» Daughter «

If you were stranded on a desert island, which three people would you want with you?

_____

_____

_____

How would these people make your experience on the island easier or better?

_____

_____

_____

_____

_____

_____

» Father «

You have been invited to a fancy party. Design an outfit to wear:

» Daughter «

You have been invited to a fancy party. Design an outfit to wear:

» Father «

What about your childhood are you most grateful for?

_____

_____

_____

_____

_____

What is something you wish had been different?

_____

_____

_____

_____

_____

» Daughter «

What are three things you are grateful for?

1 _____

_____

2 _____

_____

3 _____

_____

What is something you wish was different about your life?

_____

_____

_____

_____

_____

Father

What is the most important thing you learned in school?

_____

_____

_____

_____

_____

What are some ways that education can be improved?

_____

_____

_____

_____

_____

Daughter

What is the most important thing you've learned in school?

_____

_____

_____

_____

_____

What are some ways that you think your education could be improved?

_____

_____

_____

_____

» Father «

What would a fun father-daughter bonding night look like? What activities would you do?

_____

_____

_____

_____

Make plans to do it together! Afterward, share your thoughts on how it went. What was your favorite part?

_____

_____

_____

_____

_____

» Daughter «

What would a fun father-daughter bonding night look like? What activities would you do?

_____

_____

_____

_____

Make plans to do it together! Afterward, share your thoughts on how it went. What was your favorite part?

_____

_____

_____

_____

_____

» Father «

What are three places you'd like to travel to, and why?

1 _____

_____

_____

2 _____

_____

_____

3 _____

_____

_____

» Daughter «

What are three places you'd like to travel to, and why?

1 _____

_____

_____

2 _____

_____

_____

3 _____

_____

_____

Father

When were you most proud of your daughter?

_____

_____

_____

_____

_____

_____

_____

_____

_____

_____

» Daughter «

When was your dad most proud of you?

_____

_____

_____

_____

_____

_____

_____

_____

_____

_____